20 Answers

The Church

Trent Horn

20 Answers: The Church

Trent Horn

Published by Catholic Answers, Inc.

2020 Gillespie Way

El Cajon, California 92020

1-888-291-8000 orders

619-387-0042 fax

catholic.com

Printed in the United States of America

978-1-68357-039-4

978-1-68357-040-0 Kindle

978-1-68357-041-7 ePub

Introduction

Several years ago, I took part in a pro-life missionary trip with a mixed group of Protestants and Catholics. On Sunday, we split up to attend our respective churches, and the Catholics I was with asked one of the Protestants, whom I'll call Caleb, to join us if he liked.

The town we were visiting had a church affiliated with the denomination Caleb belonged to, but since he didn't know anyone who attended that church, he told us, "You know, I think I'm probably just going to stay with my host family and read the Bible today, but thanks for offering, guys."

My Catholic friends, who were used to going to church every Sunday unless they were sick, were baffled by this response. They asked Caleb why he thought it was okay to stay home, to which he replied, "I mean, church is great for the community and teachings, but the only thing we really need is the Bible."

It's not just certain Protestants who think the Church is not an essential element of the Christian life. According to Georgetown University, one-quarter of Catholics attend Mass only a few times a year (such as Christmas and Easter), and one-third rarely or never attend Catholic services at all. If Caleb and others like him are correct, then this shouldn't bother us, because church attendance is a helpful but nonetheless optional part of the Faith.

But what if this attitude is mistaken? After all, St. Paul spoke of the Church of God not as a helpful accessory; he instead boldly called it "the pillar and foundation of truth" (1 Tim. 3:15).

In this booklet, we will answer the most common questions people ask about the Church and show how God's plan to gather his family into one covenant finds its fulfillment in Christ's Church.

1. What is the Church?

Church is a translation of the Greek word *ekklesia*, which means "assembly" or "the called out ones."[1] In the ancient world, *ekklesia* referred to the practice of calling citizens out of their homes and into a public meeting place. For Christians, the word refers to God's people, who have been "called out" of the world for the purpose of being his "chosen ones." St. Paul put it this way: "[God] chose us in him before the foundation of the world, that we should be holy and blameless before him. He destined us in love to be his sons through Jesus Christ, according to the purpose of his will" (Eph. 1:4–5). In fact, the English word *church* comes from the German *kirche*, which means "what belongs to the Lord."

The gathering of God's people into a single assembly began in the Old Testament through the covenants made with Abraham and Moses. As the *Catechism of the Catholic Church* (CCC) puts it, this remote preparation acted as a sign for the future gathering of people from every nation into Christ's kingdom (762). For example, just as the Israelites were a kingdom of priests (Exod. 19:6), all Christians share in Christ's priesthood (1 Pet. 2:9). In addition, the ministerial priesthood of the Old Testament has continued through the successors of the apostles, or the bishops, and the priests they appoint. The *Catechism* puts it this way:

> The Lord Jesus endowed his community with a structure that will remain until the kingdom is fully achieved. Before all else there is the choice of the Twelve with Peter as their head. Representing the twelve tribes of Israel, they are the foundation stones of the new Jerusalem. The Twelve and the other disciples share in Christ's mission and his power, but also in his lot. By all his actions, Christ prepares and builds his Church (765).

One metaphor for the Church that is found throughout Scripture and helps explain this structure is the body of Christ. Some people think the Church is just a loose collection of believers contained by a minimal set of beliefs—in the same way a collection of gifts can be called "one" because all the gifts are in the same basket. But the Bible teaches that the Church is a single entity (Rom. 12:5) whose members are a part of Christ and one another (1 Cor. 12:27).

The most vivid metaphor that conveys this truth about the Church is that of the body. St. Paul taught the Christians in Ephesus that "the husband is the head of the wife as Christ is the head of the Church, his body, and is himself its savior" (Eph. 5:23). To the Christians in Corinth he likewise wrote,

> For just as the body is one and has many members, and all the members of the body, though many, are one body, so it is with Christ. For by one Spirit we were all baptized into one body—Jews or Greeks, slaves or free—and all were made to drink of one Spirit. For the body does not consist of one member but of many (1 Cor. 12:12–14).

In the time of the apostles, believers were called Christians, but the Church itself was not called "the Christian Church." It was referred to simply as "the Church," as is evident in Luke's description of what Paul and Barnabas did in the city of Antioch, located in modern Turkey. He says, "For a whole year they met with the Church, and taught a large company of people; and in Antioch the disciples were for the first time called Christians" (Acts 11:26).

Several decades later, St. Ignatius of Antioch penned a letter to Christians who lived six hundred miles away in the coastal city of Smyrna. He said, "Wherever the bishop shall appear, there let the multitude [of the people] also be; even as, wherever Jesus Christ is, there is the Catholic Church."[2] The word *Catholic* comes from the Greek word *kataholos*, which means "according to" (*kata*) "the whole" (*holos*). Christ's Church is called the Catholic Church because it is the same Church regardless of the area or time in which it is found, because it contains the fullness of God's eternal plan of salvation for the human race.

2. Is the Catholic Church the same as the church of the Bible or the church of the early Christians?

According to Scripture, Christ founded a visible church that has authority to teach and discipline believers and will never go out of existence (Matt. 16:18–19; 18:17). St. Paul tells us that this was built on "the foundation of the apostles" (Eph. 2:20) and would have a hierarchy composed of deacons (1 Tim. 2:8–13); presbyters, from which we get the English word *priest* (1 Tim. 5:17); and bishops (1 Tim. 3:1–7). Paul even instructed one of these bishops, Titus, to appoint priests on the island of Crete (Titus 1:5).

Unlike the apostles, who would eventually die, Christ's Church would remain on earth until his Second Coming. In order to accomplish this, the apostles passed their authority to bind and to loose doctrine (see Matt. 18:18), forgive sins (see John 20:23), and speak on behalf of Christ (see Luke 10:16) to their successors. Acts

1:20, for example, records how after Judas's death Peter proclaimed that Judas's office (or, as the King James Version translates it, his *bishopric*) would be transferred to a worthy successor. In 1 Timothy 5:22, Paul warned Timothy to "not be hasty in the laying on of hands" when Timothy appointed new leaders in the Church.

In A.D. 110, St. Ignatius of Antioch told his readers, "Follow the bishop, even as Jesus Christ does the Father, and the presbytery as you would the apostles; and reverence the deacons, as being the institution of God. Let no man do anything connected with the Church without the bishop."[3]

At the end of the first century, the fourth pope, Clement I, reminded the Christians in the city of Corinth about apostolic succession, saying:

> Our apostles knew through our Lord Jesus Christ that there would be strife for the office of bishop. For this reason, therefore, having received perfect foreknowledge, they appointed those who have already been mentioned and afterward added the further provision that, if they should die, other approved men should succeed to their ministry.[4]

Both the New Testament and the records of the early Church show that this succession of authority has enabled the Church to preserve the apostles' original teachings. For example, the book of Acts describes how the members of the Church "held steadfastly to the apostles' teaching and fellowship, to the breaking of the bread and to the prayers" (Acts 2:42). The *Didache*, a first-century catechism, exhorts Christians: "Assemble on the Lord's day, and break bread and offer the Eucharist; but first make confession of your faults, so that your sacrifice may be a pure one."[5]

In the second century, St. Justin Martyr wrote about the Mass and how the assembled "offer hearty prayers in common for ourselves and for the baptized [illuminated] person, and for all others in every place," and after that, they "salute one another with a kiss." The presider then takes bread and wine and does the following:

> [He] gives praise and glory to the Father of the universe, through the name of the Son and of the Holy Ghost, and offers thanks at considerable length for our being counted worthy to receive these things at his hands. And when he has concluded the prayers and thanksgivings, all the people present express their assent by saying Amen.[6]

Justin's description corresponds to the prayers of the faithful, the kiss of peace, the prayer of thanksgiving, and the great amen that are still part of Mass today. Justin goes on to say that the bread and wine at Mass are not mere symbols of Christ's body and blood, but instead "the flesh and blood of that Jesus who was made flesh."

The Anglican scholar J.N.D. Kelly said, "Eucharistic teaching, it should be understood at the outset, was in general unquestioningly realist, i.e., the consecrated bread and wine were taken to be, and were treated and designated as, the savior's body and blood."[7]

The Eucharist and the authority of the clergy are just two examples of how today's Catholic Church maintains the beliefs and practices of the ancient Church of Christ and the Apostles. Other ancient practices the Catholic Church faithfully preserves include infant baptism, confessing sins to a priest, and praying for the dead.[8] As the famous convert Cardinal John Henry Newman said, "To be deep in history is to cease to be Protestant."

3. Why don't Catholics rely on the Bible alone?

Imagine if every American had the authority to decide what the U.S. Constitution means. Each person could do as he wished, claiming that his actions fell under his own interpretation of the words in the Constitution. What would come of this approach? Anarchy. Fortunately, America's Founding Fathers created the Supreme Court to interpret the Constitution. Through the Court's decisions, a uniform legal code that binds all citizens equally was ensured.

The Protestant Reformers believed that all the truth about Christianity comes from the Bible alone, or that the Bible is our sole, infallible rule of faith. They called this principle *sola scriptura*, or "by Scripture alone," but we might call it a "blueprint for anarchy."[9] Indeed, today, we witness the proliferation of Protestant denominations that teach mutually contradictory positions on many important matters of faith. For just as personal interpretation of the Constitution would lead to chaos for the rule of law, relying solely on one's personal interpretation of the Bible as a guide to Christian doctrine leads to chaos for the rule of faith.

Interestingly, the Bible itself never asserts that all of divine revelation is found explicitly and only within its pages. The usual passage Protestants cite in favor of *sola scriptura* is 2 Timothy 3:16–17. In this letter, Paul tells his disciple Timothy how he should behave and grow as a man of God and a leader in the Church. Paul writes, "All Scripture is inspired by God and profitable for teaching, for reproof, for correction, and for training in righteousness, that the man of God may be complete, equipped for every good work."

Catholics agree that all Scripture is inspired by God and is useful for teaching and training, but this doesn't mean that Scripture is the *only* thing that is useful in this way. Neither does it mean that Scripture is the only source of God's saving revelation. Some Protestants argue that this verse does say Scripture alone is sufficient for salvation because it makes the man of God "equipped for every good work." But elsewhere, Paul describes other things that equip a man to do "every good work"—things that are not a Christian's sole source of doctrine. For example, in 2 Timothy 2:21, Paul says that if Timothy cleanses himself from bad influences, he will be a vessel ready for "every good work," but that doesn't mean that Timothy's prudence will cause him to know all the essential doctrines of the Faith.

In addition, if "every good work" refers to all essential doctrines, then how could Scripture equip the man of God to know what is and is not Scripture? After all, the Bible does not have an inspired table of contents, and some Protestants have even said the canon of Scripture could be a "fallible list" of infallible books.[10] But if the Catholic Church has divine authority from Christ, then we don't have to say the Bible "just is." We can say the Church has the power to recognize and pronounce the true canon of Scripture, which it did at the synod in Rome (382) and the regional councils of Hippo (393) and Carthage (397).

Christians revere the Word of God in its written form (Sacred Scripture) and its oral form (Sacred Tradition). St. Paul commended the Corinthians for holding fast to traditions he taught (1 Cor. 11:2) and told the Thessalonians to do the same (2 Thess. 2:15). The *Catechism* says: "The Church, to whom the transmission and interpretation of revelation is entrusted, does not derive its certainty about all revealed truths from the holy scriptures alone. Both Scripture and Tradition must be accepted and honored with equal sentiments of devotion and reverence" (82).

In the second century, St. Irenaeus served as a witness to this handing on of apostolic tradition when he said that "while the languages of the world are diverse, nevertheless, the authority of the tradition is one and the same." He also rhetorically asked his readers, "For how should it be if the apostles themselves had not left us writings? Would it not be necessary, to follow the course of the tradition which they handed down to those to whom they did commit the churches?"[11]

St. Vincent of Lerins made this point in the fifth century when he noticed that heretics could cite Scripture just as well as the faithful, and so another authority was necessary—one that had been entrusted with the sacred traditions associated with interpreting Scripture. Vincent said, "It is very necessary, on account of so great intricacies of such various error, that the rule for the right understanding of the prophets and apostles should be framed in accordance with the standard of ecclesiastical and Catholic interpretation."[12]

4. Don't all Christians belong to one invisible church? Why do I need to join a specific church?

There is a sense in which "the Church" exists as the invisible bond of unity among all baptized Christians, which include Catholics, Protestants, and the Eastern

Orthodox. But that is not the same as saying the Church just *is* this invisible bond of unity. According to the Congregation for the Doctrine of the Faith (CDF), "The Christian faithful are therefore not permitted to imagine that the Church of Christ is nothing more than a collection—divided, yet in some way one—of churches and ecclesial communities."[13] The CDF went on to say that the faithful can't say the one Church of Christ doesn't really exist or that it is merely a goal toward which all Christians should strive. They must instead acknowledge that "the elements of this already-given Church exist, found in their fullness in the Catholic Church."[14]

The Second Vatican Council taught that this one Church of Christ,

> constituted and organized in the world as a society, *subsists in the Catholic Church* [emphasis added], which is governed by the successor of Peter and by the bishops in communion with him, although many elements of sanctification and of truth are found outside of its visible structure. These elements, as gifts belonging to the Church of Christ, are forces impelling toward catholic unity.[15]

Some may wonder why the Council Fathers used the phrase "subsists in the Catholic Church" rather than "is the Catholic Church" in this paragraph. This was done to affirm that non-Catholic Christian churches can contain true doctrines. They are also capable of bringing about sanctification, or an increase in holiness, among their members. One example of this would be Eastern Orthodox churches, since they have valid holy orders and valid sacraments such as the Eucharist. However, since they do not recognize the unique authority of the pope as well as other important doctrines, they are considered separated brethren who are only in partial communion with Christ's Church. The CDF said in 2007:

> It is possible, according to Catholic doctrine, to affirm correctly that the Church of Christ is present and operative in the churches and ecclesial communities not yet fully in communion with the Catholic Church, on account of the elements of sanctification and truth that are present in them.[16]

The term "ecclesial communities" refers to denominations that came into existence as a result of the Protestant Reformation. Unlike the Eastern Orthodox, or even Anglicans in the seventeenth century, these denominations lack a valid priesthood, and so they cannot confer the sacrament of the Eucharist, which is the source and summit of the Christian life (see answer 5). Even though these Christians do not belong to churches in the proper sense of the word, the CDF acknowledged that "those who are baptized in these [ecclesial] communities are, by baptism, incorporated in Christ and thus are in a certain communion, albeit imperfect, with the Church."[17]

The Catholic Church acknowledges what is holy and true in other Christian communities, but it does not let these things undercut the necessity of evangelizing our separated brethren. Indeed, it would be unloving to withhold the saving power of the sacraments for fear that the Church's teaching on these matters may offend those who disagree. As Pope St. John Paul II said, "Ecumenism is directed precisely to making the partial communion existing between Christians grow toward full communion in truth and charity."[18] The next answers will also show that only through the Catholic Church can a person receive the fullness of Christ's grace in the Eucharist as well as have confidence that he is receiving the faith of the apostles.

5. Why must Catholics go to church every Sunday?

Both Catholics and Protestants would agree that at any church, Christ is present in the people gathered there (Matt. 18:20). He is also present in the Scripture that is heard and preached. However, Catholics believe that Christ is present in their services in a unique, physical way that creates a moral obligation not found in other Protestant denominations to attend church. Specifically, at the Catholic Mass, Christ's body and blood are offered up as a sacrifice under the form of bread and wine. The *Catechism* says, "The Eucharist is the efficacious sign and sublime cause of that communion in the divine life and that unity of the people of God by which the Church is kept in being" (1325).

The name of this sacrifice, or "Eucharist," comes from the Greek word *eucharistein*, which means "thanksgiving." Like baptism and confession, the Eucharist is a sacrament—an outward expression of an inward reception of grace. The Eucharist differs from the other sacraments in an important way because it is "'the source and summit of the Christian life.' The other sacraments, and indeed all ecclesiastical ministries and works of the apostolate, are bound up with the Eucharist and are oriented toward it" (CCC 1324).

The *Catechism* goes on to say, "For in the blessed Eucharist is contained the whole spiritual good of the Church, namely Christ himself, our Pasch" (1324). The word *pasch* refers to the Jewish celebration of Passover, and it is no coincidence that the Eucharist commemorates the Passover meal Christ held with his disciples before his crucifixion. But the Eucharist is our new Passover and re-presents the sacrifice of the "Lamb of God, who takes away the sins of the world" (John 1:29). In addition, just as the lamb of the old Passover was consumed, Christ, the new Passover lamb, must also be consumed. This is why the Eucharist is also called the "Lord's Supper" or the "Breaking of Bread."

This new Passover sacrifice is offered in the context of the Mass, a term that refers to "the sending forth (*missio*) of the faithful, so that they may fulfill God's will in their daily lives" (CCC 1332). Catholics have an obligation to attend Mass on Sundays as well as on holy days of obligation, such as Christmas and All Saints' Day, because Christ told us to keep the commandments (Matt 19:17). The *Catechism* says:

> The celebration of Sunday observes the moral commandment inscribed by nature in the human heart to render to God an outward, visible, public, and regular worship "as a sign of his universal beneficence to all." . . . The Sunday Eucharist is the foundation and confirmation of all Christian practice. For this reason the faithful are obliged to participate in the Eucharist on days of obligation, unless excused for a serious reason (for example, illness, the care of infants) or dispensed by their own pastor. Those who deliberately fail in this obligation commit a grave sin (2176, 2181).

It's important to remember that the obligation to attend Mass on Sundays and holy days is distinct from the obligation to receive the Eucharist. The Church requires a person to receive the Eucharist only once a year, during the Easter season, "unless [this precept] is fulfilled for a just cause at another time during the year," per canon law. No one is obligated to receive the Eucharist at any particular Mass, because a person may be in a state of mortal sin or otherwise unable to receive. But even if a person cannot receive the Eucharist physically, he can still make an act of *spiritual* communion and pray to receive Jesus into his heart. St. Teresa of Avila said this "is a most beneficial practice; by it the love of God will be greatly impressed on you."[19]

6. Does Christ's Church need a pope?

Just as the apostles' authority was passed on to their successors, Peter's authority as the leader of the apostles was passed on to his successor. This man inherited the keys to the kingdom of heaven (see Matt. 16:18–19) and Peter's duty to shepherd Christ's flock (see John 21:15–17). Peter's successor was the pastor of Christ's Church and a spiritual father to the Lord's children (1 Cor. 4:15), thus explaining his office's future title, *pope*, which comes from *papa*, meaning "father."

Peter's role as "chief apostle" is evident in the facts that the New Testament mentions him more than any other apostle, that he often speaks for the whole group, and that he is placed first in every list of the apostles. Moreover, Christ made Peter alone the shepherd over his whole flock (see John 21:15–17), and the book of Acts describes Peter's unparalleled leadership in the early Church. This includes his authority to make a binding, dogmatic declaration at the council of Jerusalem (Acts 15). According to J.N.D. Kelly, "Peter was the undisputed leader of the youthful church."[20]

Finally, in Matthew 16:18–19, Jesus changed Simon's name to Peter, which means "rock," and said, "You are Peter [rock], and on this rock I will build my church, and the powers of death shall not prevail against it. I will give you the keys of the kingdom of heaven, and whatever you bind on earth shall be bound in heaven, and whatever you loose on earth shall be loosed in heaven."

This passage is an allusion to Isaiah 22:22, which tells of how Israel's wicked chief steward, Shebna, was replaced with the righteous Eliakim. Isaiah 22:22 says Eliakim would have "the key of the house of David; he shall open, and none shall shut; and he shall shut, and none shall open." Just as King Hezekiah gave Eliakim authority to oversee the kingdom of Israel, Christ gave Peter authority (the "keys to the kingdom") to oversee his Church, which included the authority to "bind and loose"—in other words, to determine official doctrine and practice.[21]

According to John 1:42, Jesus gave Simon the Aramaic name *Kepha*, which means simply "rock." But unlike in Aramaic, in Greek, the word *rock* is a feminine noun, so Matthew used the masculine version of *rock*, or *petros*, since calling Peter *Petras* would have been on par with calling him Patricia! The Lutheran theologian Oscar Cullman wrote, "petra=Kepha=petros,"[22] and even the Protestant Reformer John Calvin said, "There is no difference of meaning, I acknowledge, between the two Greek words *petros* and *petra*."[23]

Finally, if Peter is not the rock upon whom the Church is built, then why did Jesus bother to change Simon's name in the first place? As Protestant scholar Craig Keener writes in his commentary on Matthew, "[Jesus] plays on Simon's nickname, 'Peter,' which is roughly the English 'Rocky': Peter is 'rocky,' and on this rock Jesus would build his Church."[24]

With regard to the authority of Peter's successors, or those who served as bishop of Rome, in the first century, Clement of Rome (the fourth pope) intervened in a dispute in the church of Corinth (a Greek city west of Athens). He warned those who disobeyed him that they would "involve themselves in transgression and in no small danger," thus demonstrating his authority over non-Roman Christians.[25] St. Ignatius of Antioch referred to the Roman church as the one that teaches other churches and "presides in love" over them.[26] In fact, the writings of Pope Clement (A.D. 92–99) and Pope Soter (A.D. 167–174) were so popular that they were read in the Church alongside Scripture.[27] In A.D. 190, Pope St. Victor I excommunicated an entire region of churches for refusing to celebrate Easter on its proper date. Some of his contemporaries, such as St. Irenaeus, thought this was not prudent, but none of them denied that Victor had the authority to do it.

Keep in mind that all of this evidence dates a hundred to two hundred years before Christianity was legalized in the Roman Empire, thus deflating the anti-Catholic theory that the Roman emperor created the papacy in the fourth century (see answer 11).

7. What is papal infallibility?

The doctrine of papal infallibility teaches that the pope has a special grace from Christ that protects him from leading the Church into error. That grace won't keep him from sinning (even gravely), nor will it give him the right answer to every issue facing the Church. Instead, it will protect the pope from officially leading the Church into heresy. As a private theologian, the pope might speculate, even incorrectly, about the Faith, but he will never issue a false teaching related to faith or morality that claims to be binding and infallible (or an erroneous *ex cathedra* teaching).

But why believe that the pope is infallible? Matthew 16:18 says the "powers of death"—in Greek, "the gates of Hades," or hell—will never prevail against the Church, so it makes sense that the pastor of Christ's Church will never steer it into hell by teaching heresy. Luke 22:31–32 records Jesus telling Peter, "Satan has demanded to sift you all like wheat, but I have prayed for you that your faith may not fail; and when you have turned again, strengthen your brethren." The original

Greek in the passage shows that Satan demanded to sift "you all," or all the apostles, but Jesus prayed only for Peter and Peter's faith not to fail.

Now, it's true that Christ once called Peter "Satan" for trying to stop the Crucifixion (Matt. 16:23), and he knew that Peter would later deny him at his trial. But God doesn't call the perfect—he perfects the called. Christ prayed that once Peter had "turned again" from his sins, he would lead and strengthen the apostles. Jesus even appeared to Peter first after the Resurrection (1 Cor. 15:5).

No one denies that some popes engaged in serious sins, such as fornication, but infallibility means only that the pope won't teach error, not that he will be sinless (that's called *impeccability*). For example, St. Paul opposed Peter in Antioch and said he was wrong or "stood condemned" (Gal. 2:11–14). But in this situation, Peter, at most, made an error in behavior, not teaching. Peter feared antagonism from Christians who thought circumcision was necessary for salvation. So, while he was in their presence, Peter declined to eat with the uncircumcised. Paul criticized Peter's actions, but he did not question Peter's teachings or accuse him of spreading heresy.

Indeed, some Church Fathers, such as St. Cyprian of Carthage, criticized the pope's decisions, but even Cyprian believed that the pope could not lead the Church astray. He wrote in A.D. 256 of heretics who dared approach "the throne of Peter . . . to whom faithlessness could have no access," or, as other translations put it, "from whom no error can flow."[28]

Ironically, when well-read Protestants claim that certain popes taught error, they pass over the tabloid-worthy medieval popes. They agree that even though a few of those popes *engaged in debauchery*, none of them *taught heresy*. However, the examples they cite typically involve a pope cowardly tolerating heresy and not one officially teaching it. For example, it's true that the Third Council of Constantinople (680) said Pope Honorius I (625–638) was a heretic, but only in the sense that Honorius failed to curb the Monothelite heresy, not in the sense that he endorsed it as an article of faith for the Church.

The Monothelites taught that Christ had only a divine will and not a corresponding human will. But even Jaroslav Pelikan, a renowned non-Catholic scholar of Church history, admits that Honorius's opposition to the idea that Christ had two wills "was based on the interpretation of 'two wills' as 'two contrary wills.' He did not mean that Christ was an incomplete human being."[29] A good resource on this subject is Patrick Madrid's book *Pope Fiction*, which contains an overview of Honorius as well as other popes accused of being heretics.

8. Is the Church infallible?

According to the *Catechism*, "The pastoral duty of the Magisterium is aimed at seeing to it that the people of

God abides in the truth that liberates. To fulfill this service, Christ endowed the Church's shepherds with the charism of infallibility in matters of faith and morals" (890).

We've already seen how the gift of infallibility is given to the pope when he proclaims by a definitive act a dogma pertaining to faith or morals. Two examples of this kind of infallibility are Pope Pius IX's definition of the Immaculate Conception and Pope Pius XII's definition of Mary's bodily assumption into heaven. Both dogmatic definitions are infallible and unchangeable, but such dogmas do not only spring forth from papal declarations (or *ex cathedra* teachings). The *Catechism* says:

> "The infallibility promised to the Church is also present in the body of bishops when, together with Peter's successor, they exercise the supreme Magisterium," above all in an Ecumenical Council [see answer 10]. When the Church through its supreme Magisterium proposes a doctrine "for belief as being divinely revealed," and as the teaching of Christ, the definitions "must be adhered to with the obedience of faith." This infallibility extends as far as the deposit of divine revelation itself (891).

Doctrines of this kind are called dogmas, and they are the central truths of the Faith. As such, they demand our most committed level of belief, or what is called *the assent of faith*. The CDF says, concerning the dogmas of the Church, "Whoever obstinately places them in doubt or denies them falls under the censure of heresy, as indicated by the respective canons of the Codes of Canon Law."[30]

According to the *Catechism*:

> The Church's Magisterium exercises the authority it holds from Christ to the fullest extent when it defines dogmas, that is, when it proposes, in a form obliging the Christian people to an irrevocable adherence of faith, truths contained in divine revelation or also when it proposes, in a definitive way, truths having a necessary connection with these (88).

A teaching is a dogma if (1) it binds the faithful to believe it with the assent or adherence of faith and (2) it comes from divine revelation. All dogmas are definitive and infallible, but not all definitive and infallible teachings are dogmas. Some have a necessary connection to divine revelation but are not explicitly found within the Deposit of Faith. Examples of this kind of infallible, non-dogmatic teaching are the Church's pronouncement that a certain pope was validly elected or that an ecumenical council was validly convened. There is nothing in divine revelation that speaks about popes or general councils from after the apostolic age, but these truths have a necessary connection to the dogma of the Church's general infallibility found in divine revelation.

We must remember that, according to canon law (the *Codex Iuris Canonici*, or CIC), a teaching is not infallible unless the Church explicitly says it is infallible (CIC 749.3). A teaching can be defined as an infallible dogma by the pope speaking in his capacity as the successor of St. Peter (such as when Pope Pius XII defined the dogma of Mary's bodily assumption). It can also be defined by the ordinary and universal teaching authority of the Church, such as the universal witness in ecclesial documents that killing innocent human beings is wrong. Or it can be defined through the canons of an ecumenical council (see answer 10).

For example, the teaching that Christ's body, blood, soul, and divinity are truly present in the Eucharist is a dogma of the Faith that was divinely revealed to the Church. It was defined in the sixteenth century at the Council of Trent, but the dogma was believed long before that time. It is well attested to in Sacred Scripture and Sacred Tradition. The dogma was defined at the Council of Trent only because such an act was necessary to counter heresies related to the Eucharist that emerged during the Protestant Reformation.

Some critics claim that the Church is not infallible because it has changed some teachings that were supposedly unchangeable. A common claim is that prior to the Second Vatican Council, the Church condemned religious freedom, but after the council, it embraced tolerance for other religions. This argument fails to understand the changing nature of the issues in question.

Prior to the council, religious freedom was synonymous with religious indifferentism and the idea that no one, including the Church, could insist that a person think a certain way about religious truths. In 1864, Pope Pius IX condemned the idea that "a right resides in the citizens to an absolute liberty, which should be restrained by no authority whether ecclesiastical or civil."[31] The Second Vatican Council was not arguing for religious indifferentism. Instead, the Council Fathers said religious freedom means that "all men are to be immune from coercion on the part of individuals or of social groups and of any human power."[32]

In short, false ideas don't have a right to exist (as the Church taught before Vatican II), but people have the right to believe something even if it turns out to be false. This includes the freedom to believe they ought not to become Catholic, which is evident in the Church's denunciation of forced baptisms that some individuals carried out in the Middle Ages.[33]

9. What is the difference between a dogma, a doctrine, and a discipline?

Doctrine is that teaching the Church proposes for the faithful to believe and can refer to an individual teaching (a doctrine) or to the totality of all the Church's teachings (Catholic doctrine). Some of these teachings are dogmas, which the Church infallibly defines as divinely revealed teachings that the faithful are obliged to believe. We must remember that even though every dogma of the Faith is a doctrine, most doctrines are not dogmas, nor are they infallibly defined. They can be changed or clarified, and so they require "religious submission of mind and will" rather than the "assent of faith."

So, for example, the *Catechism* says, "The Church teaches that every spiritual soul is created immediately by God—it is not 'produced' by the parents—and also that it is immortal: it does not perish when it separates from the body at death, and it will be reunited with the body at the final resurrection" (366). That human beings have immortal souls is a dogma of the Church that was infallibly defined at the Fifth Lateran Council in 1513 (it has also been part of the continual, universal teaching of the Church, or the "ordinary magisterium"). That God creates those souls directly, however, is a doctrine rather than a dogma. The Church could declare this to be a dogma in the future, but for now it is a doctrine because it has not been infallibly defined as being divinely revealed.

The faithful cannot openly dissent against any doctrine, but unlike with dogmas, it is not a grave sin to personally fail to accept them. Still, it is a serious matter to withhold the submission of the mind and will, and the Church usually speaks of theologians who, after careful study, cautiously do this with the aim of helping the Magisterium better understand a disputed issue.[34]

The difference between the assent of faith and the religious submission of mind and will is not a license for lay Catholics to reject any non-infallible teachings they simply do not like. It is instead a recognition that the Church does not always make its teaching definitive, but the faithful should still trust in the shepherds Christ has left us even as they, under the guidance of the Holy Spirit, further clarify and present the Faith handed on to them that they pass on to us.

Before we examine the Church's disciplines, we must distinguish doctrine from theological opinions. A teaching is a doctrine if the Church proposes it for belief among the faithful, even if it is not infallible in nature. However, there are theological issues and questions to which the Church has not proposed a definitive answer. There will be no new public revelation that will answer these questions (CCC 66), but the Church may develop a deeper understanding of the Faith and, consequently, propose a doctrine in response.

One example of a theological opinion is the state of Mary's body upon her assumption into heaven. While the fact that Mary's body was assumed into heaven is a dogma of the Church, the Church has not weighed in on the question of whether Mary was assumed before or after death. In his apostolic constitution that defined the dogma, Pope Pius XII said only that "the ever Virgin Mary, having completed the course of her earthly life, was assumed body and soul into heavenly glory."[35] Notice how the pope spoke only of the end of Mary's earthly life and not of the manner in which it ended. Although most theologians, past and present, have speculated that Mary's body was assumed after death, a Catholic can believe she was assumed either before or after her death (the latter is the more traditional view).

This leaves us with disciplines, which are the rules and laws the Church proposes by the authority given to it by Christ. Even though disciplines can be changed, the faithful are still obliged to obey them, just as citizens must obey speed limits that a municipal government can change when it deems it necessary.

An example of a discipline is the communion fast. For most of Church history, the faithful fasted from midnight until they received the Eucharist that morning. Only after that would they have a meal that would "break the fast" (i.e., breakfast). However, in 1953, Pope Pius XII reduced the period of fasting to three hours before Communion to encourage greater reception of the sacrament.[36] In 1964, Pope Paul VI changed the period of fasting once again, this time to one hour before Communion. The current *Code of Canon Law* says, "A person who is to receive the Most Holy Eucharist is to abstain for at least one hour before holy communion from any food and drink, except for only water and medicine" (CIC 919).

To summarize, doctrine refers to all the teachings or beliefs the Church proposes for the faithful to believe. Dogmas are a subset of doctrines that are unchangeable and, because they are a part of divine revelation, require the assent of faith. Disciplines come from the Church and must be obeyed even though the Magisterium can alter or abolish them.

10. What is an ecumenical council?

Each bishop has authority over his particular church, but when the bishops of the world teach in union with the pope, they possess authority over the entire Church. Through ecumenical councils, the bishops gather, usually in the face of popular heresies and cultural challenges, in order to clarify doctrine and define what the faithful are obliged to believe. According to the *Catechism*, "The college of bishops exercises power over the universal Church in a solemn manner in an ecumenical council. But there never is an ecumenical council which is not confirmed or at least recognized as such by Peter's successor" (884). This tradition can be found in Scripture when the Apostles met in Jerusalem and, through Peter's revelation and teaching, declared that Gentile converts do not have to be circumcised (Acts 15:1–29).

Since the Church's beginning, there have been twenty-one ecumenical councils, with the following being some of the most noteworthy:

The First Council of Nicaea (325)
Repudiated the heresy of Arianism, which claimed that Christ is not equal in divinity with the Father. The canons of this council and the first council of Constantinople (381) form the basis of the Nicene Creed that Catholics recite every Sunday.

The Council of Ephesus (431)
Rejected the heresy of Nestorianism and declared that Christ is one person with two natures, one fully human and the other fully divine. This council dogmatically defined that Mary is *Theotokos*, or the Mother of God.

The Council of Chalcedon (451)
Condemned the heresy of Monophysitism, which claimed that Christ has only one (divine) nature (or one nature that is part divine and part human). The council's teaching on the person and nature of Jesus Christ is considered a foundational element of modern Christology.

The Second Council of Nicaea (787)
Condemned the heresy of iconoclasm and deemed it

appropriate to venerate holy images, including those depicting members of the Trinity, so long as the images aren't given the worship due to God alone.

Both the Catholic Church and Eastern Orthodox churches recognize the authority of the first seven ecumenical councils. Protestants, on the other hand, see these councils as valuable historic witnesses to the Christian faith and generally abide by their teachings, but they reject the idea that these councils have authority over believers today. In fact, only Catholics acknowledge the authority of the remaining fourteen ecumenical councils, some of the most notable being:

The Fourth Council of the Lateran (1215)
Dogmatically defined transubstantiation, or the miracle by which bread and wine become the body and blood of Christ in the Eucharist offered at Mass.

The Council of Constance (1414–1418)
Sanctioned early Protestant heretics and resolved a dispute over the papacy called the Great Western Schism.

The Council of Trent (1545–1563)
Repudiated the heresy of Protestantism and clarified the Church's teachings on Scripture, justification, and the nature of the sacraments.

The First Vatican Council (1870)
Condemned modern heresies and defined the dogma of papal infallibility.

The Second Vatican Council (1962–1965)
Addressed the relationship between the Church and the modern world, especially concerning the liturgy, the nature of divine revelation, and the role of ecumenism.

11. Did the Catholic Church emerge from paganism in the fourth century?

Some people claim that the Catholic Church came into existence in the early part of the fourth century after the Roman emperor Constantine converted to Christianity. Reformed writer Lorraine Boettner presents one such scenario:

> In the fourth century the emperor Constantine, who was the ruler in the West, began to favor Christianity, and then in the year 324, after he had become ruler of all the empire, made Christianity the official religion. The result was that thousands of people who were still pagans pressed into the church in order to gain the special advantages that went with such membership. . . . Gradually, through the neglect of the Bible and the ignorance

> of the people, more and more heathen ideas were introduced until the church became more heathen than Christian.[37]

There are two glaring errors in Boettner's revisionist view of Church history. First, Emperor Constantine did not make Christianity the official religion of the Roman Empire. Constantine did enact the Edict of Milan in 313, but that only granted legal toleration for the Faith. Christianity did not become the official religion of the empire until the reign of the Roman emperor Theodosius I in 380.

Second, Boettner ignores the fact that "heathen ideas" such as the real presence of Christ in the Eucharist and the necessity of baptism can be found in the works of early Christian writers such as Justin, Irenaeus, Cyprian, and Tertullian, who all lived long before Constantine's reign. For example, even Protestant scholars admit that the doctrine of baptismal regeneration, or the teaching that baptism removes the stain of original sin, was adhered to long before the time of Emperor Constantine. According to Reformed apologist William Webster:

> The doctrine of baptism is one of the few teachings within Roman Catholicism for which it can be said that there is a universal consent of the Fathers. . . . From the early days of the Church, baptism

> was universally perceived as the means of receiving four basic gifts: the remission of sins, deliverance from death, regeneration, and the bestowal of the Holy Spirit.[38]

Critics like Boettner also fail to understand that the Church, guided by the Holy Spirit, is capable of baptizing pagan rites and using them in service of the gospel. This is called inculturation, which Pope St. John Paul II describes in this way:

> Through inculturation the Church makes the gospel incarnate in different cultures and at the same time introduces peoples, together with their cultures, into its own community. It transmits to them its own values, at the same time taking the good elements that already exist in them and renewing them from within. Through inculturation the Church, for its part, becomes a more intelligible sign of what it is, and a more effective instrument of mission.[39]

In the nineteenth century, Cardinal John Henry Newman admitted that many rituals in the Church have a non-Christian origin. The following quote attributed to him can be found on several anti-Catholic websites: "Temples, incense, oil lamps, votive offerings, holy water, holidays and seasons of devotions, processions, blessing of fields, sacerdotal vestments, the tonsure (of priests and monks and nuns), images . . . are all of pagan origin."[40]

Notice how this quote contains a carefully placed ellipsis, which indicates that a portion of the quote has been excised. The missing part contains the phrase "the ring in marriage," which was left out because Protestants routinely engage in this custom during their wedding services. The Bible says nothing of wedding rings, but they were common in places such as ancient Egypt because they symbolized eternity and were worn on the finger that purportedly contained a nerve that extended all the way to the heart.[41]

If the Catholic customs of using incense, candles, and chants contain an unforgivable infusion of "heathenism" into the Church, then Protestant churches that use fog machines, stage lights, and rock music contain a heathen infusion, too. Baptist harvest festivals celebrated on or just after Halloween are another example of Protestant inculturation, since they feature morally good or neutral activities, such as communal fall festivities and giving out candy, without endorsing morally evil things, such as the occult. John Paul II taught that using cultural elements in service of the gospel is not wrong as long as such elements "in no way compromise the distinctiveness and integrity of the Christian faith."[42]

12. Did the Catholic Church begin in the eleventh century after the "Great Schism"?

The Great Schism refers to a series of events that led to the separation of many Eastern churches from the Catholic Church, which resulted in the genesis of the Eastern Orthodox churches. The Orthodox bishop Timothy Ware (also known as Kallistos Ware) says, "The schism, as historians now generally recognize, is not really an event whose beginning can be exactly dated. It was something that came about gradually, as the result of a long and complicated process, starting well before the eleventh century and not completed until some time after."[43]

Over the course of several centuries, the Eastern and Western elements of the Church grew apart as they began to speak different languages (Latin in the West, Greek in the East), abide by different customs, vary in their expression of different doctrines, and fall under the rules of different emperors. Through all of this, the East and West were still united as the Catholic Church. This changed, however, in the middle of the eleventh century, when the patriarch of Constantinople and a cardinal representing the pope met to discuss the patriarch's requirement that Latin churches in his region abandon their Western customs (such as using unleavened bread at Mass) and adopt Eastern traditions instead. Rather than reach a compromise, the meeting ended with each party excommunicating the other.

This event became a turning point in the East's separation from the West, but it did not mark the formal beginning of the schism. That formal beginning came about as the East grew more and more resentful of the West, especially after the emperor of Byzantium persuaded Crusaders from the West to help him recover his throne from his uncle, who had usurped it in a coup. According to Ware, eventually, the Crusaders lost patience with what they regarded as Greek duplicity and sacked Constantinople. "Eastern Christendom has never forgotten those three appalling days of pillage. . . . After 1204 there can be no doubt that Christian East and Christian West were divided into two."[44]

So what are the differences between the Catholic Church and the Eastern Orthodox? Some are purely related to discipline and so do not justify schism, since Eastern *Catholic* churches also practice many, if not most, of the disciplines found among the Eastern Orthodox. Remember that Christ established one Church, but within that Church are communities that have retained different traditions and celebrate the liturgy in different ways (or according to different rites). The Western Church is well known for the Latin rite, whose membership is larger than the other twenty-three rites put together. But amid the different traditions and customs in these rites (Eastern Catholics call the Mass "the Divine Liturgy," for example), all of these Catholic churches are united in professing the same Faith. According to the Second Vatican Council:

> Variety within the Church in no way harms its unity; rather it manifests it, for it is the mind of the Catholic Church that each individual church or rite should retain its traditions whole and entire . . . although they differ somewhat among themselves in rite (to use the current phrase), that is, in liturgy, ecclesiastical discipline, and spiritual heritage, [they] are, nevertheless, each as much as the others, entrusted to the pastoral government of the Roman pontiff, the divinely appointed successor of St. Peter in primacy over the universal Church."[45]

For example, Byzantine Catholic churches, which can be found throughout Eastern Europe as well as among immigrant communities in the U.S. and other countries, use leavened bread in their liturgies. They also follow the Eastern practice of administering the Eucharist to infants after they have received confirmation (or what is called chrismation). But, unlike Eastern Orthodox churches, they affirm the same doctrines as Latin-rite Catholics and recognize the supreme authority of the pope. Eastern Orthodox churches differ significantly on these points, especially on the doctrines of the Trinity and the papacy.

With regard to the Trinity, centuries of theological discussion have brought Catholics and Eastern Orthodox closer together on the subject. The main point of disagreement is the *filioque* clause in the Creed, which says the Holy Spirit proceeds from the Father "and the Son." Eastern Orthodox say the Holy Spirit proceeds solely from the Father, but if one understands that everything the Son has ultimately comes from the Father who begot him, then these two formulations can be equally accurate. According to the *Catechism*, "This legitimate complementarity, provided it does not become rigid, does not affect the identity of faith in the reality of the same mystery confessed" (248).

With regard to the papacy, it is not true that the Catholic Church and its belief in the primacy and infallibility of the bishop of Rome sprang *ex nihilo* from the eleventh century. As we've seen, there is evidence from ancient witnesses in the West and the East who recognized the primacy and authority of the bishop of Rome. In the fourth century, the ecumenical Council of Constantinople declared that "the bishop of Constantinople shall have the primacy of honor after the bishop of Rome, because his city is New Rome" (canon 3). Constantinople was called "new Rome" because of Emperor Constantine's decision to move the imperial capital there, but the patriarchs in the region understood that their authority was still under the primacy of Rome, because the bishop of Rome is the successor of St. Peter.

13. Did the Church become corrupt during the Middle Ages, thus necessitating the Protestant Reformation?

A true reformation of the Church would involve eliminating abuses and errors that hampered the Church's mission of preaching the gospel. What the so-called Reformers offered instead was a *rejection* of the Catholic Church's authority. In its place, they held up the Bible, along with their unique interpretation of it, as a Christian's sole infallible rule of faith.

According to Protestant historian Alister McGrath:

> [Martin] Luther demanded that all Christians should be able to read the Bible for themselves. The agenda here was both political and theological. Lay access to the Bible was about power as much as it was about encouraging personal spirituality. Pressure for the Bible to be placed in the hands of the ordinary person was an implicit demand for the emancipation of the laity from clerical domination.[46]

Unfortunately, instead of strengthening Christ's Church, the Reformers' "Bible only" approach has led to the formation of hundreds, if not thousands, of competing Protestant denominations. These churches disagree even over crucial issues such as the validity of infant baptism, the real presence of Christ in the Eucharist, and whether believers can lose their salvation.

True reform of Christ's Church came not from men like Luther or Calvin, but from the faithful bishops who implemented changes instituted by the ecumenical Council of Trent in 1563. These reforms included the formation of seminaries to ensure the proper education of priests. They also included changes to the liturgy to make it more accessible for laypeople (such as permitting the reception of the Eucharist under either the form of bread or the form of wine).

Another example involves indulgences, which, contrary to myths, are not tickets to heaven that the Church sold. Instead, indulgences were, and still are, a way for the Church to remove the temporal effects of sin from our souls as opposed to having those effects removed after death in purgatory.

How do indulgences accomplish this?

The Church teaches that the holiness of some can be applied to the benefit of others. For example, Paul said the Jews of his time were "beloved for the sake of their forefathers" (Rom. 11:28), and God delayed the destruction of the city of Sodom and spared some its population because of Abraham's intercession (Gen. 18). It follows, therefore, that the merits of Christ, which were infinitely more than what was necessary to take away the sin of the world, as well as the merits of the saints in heaven, can be applied to the sufferings of believers on earth and even the suffering of believers in purgatory. The *Catechism* says:

> The "treasury of the Church" is the infinite value, which can never be exhausted, which Christ's merits have before God. They were offered so that the whole of mankind could be set free from sin and attain communion with the Father. . . . In the treasury, too, are the prayers and good works of all the saints, all those who have followed in the footsteps of Christ the Lord and by his grace have made their lives holy and carried out the mission in the unity of the Mystical Body (1476–77).

Indulgences are the Church's way of applying the treasury of merits to individuals in order to "obtain from the Father of mercies the remission of the temporal punishment due for their sins" (CCC 1478). The Church has this authority because Christ told the apostles that they have the ability to forgive sins (John 20:23) and that whatever they bind on earth shall be bound in heaven, and whatever they loose on earth shall be loosed in heaven (Matt. 18:18).

Since nothing unclean can enter heaven (Rev. 21:27), and the sacrament of confession remits only the eternal punishment for sins, it follows that there must be another way to purge the temporal effect of sin as well as our unhealthy attachment to sin before we enter heaven. One way this is accomplished is through indulgences, which can be obtained for one's own sins or on behalf of another.

An indulgence can be obtained by performing a good work associated with it (for example, going on a pilgrimage) while also being in a state of grace, being completely detached from sin, going to confession, receiving the Eucharist, and praying for the intentions of the pope. Prior to the Council of Trent, one good work that could be performed was the giving of alms, since, as Scripture says, love and almsgiving in particular cover a multitude of sins (Tob. 4:10; 1 Pet. 4:8).

However, some people treated this good work as a crude transaction, where they simply gave their surplus money in exchange for the remission of sins. Because of the potential for abuse, almsgiving was removed from the process of obtaining an indulgence. However, the practice of receiving indulgences was not removed and continues in the Church today. The faithful can even obtain indulgences on behalf of the deceased in purgatory in order to help them in their process of purification (CCC 1479).

14. How can the Church be called holy, given its past crimes?

The Church is holy not because its members are perfect, but because of Christ, who, according to the *Catechism*, "'loved the Church as his Bride, giving himself up for her so as to sanctify her; he joined her to himself as his body and endowed her with the gift of the Holy Spirit for the glory of God.' The Church, then, is 'the holy people of God,' and her members are called 'saints'" (823). There no contradiction in calling the Church holy because it is the means through which God sanctifies sinners and admitting that all people, including Catholics, are sinners in need of God's grace. Pope Paul VI put it this way:

> The Church is therefore holy, though having sinners in its midst, because it itself has no other life but the life of grace. If they live its life, its members are sanctified; if they move away from its life, they fall into sins and disorders that prevent the radiation of its sanctity. This is why it suffers and does penance for those offenses, of which it has the power to free its children through the blood of Christ and the gift of the Holy Spirit.[47]

Although it is true that some Catholics, including bishops and popes, have sinned grievously, it is also true that some allegations against the Church are exaggerated or flat-out false. Here are just a few examples:

Stifling Science

Those who make the claim that the Church is anti-science forget that after the destruction of the Roman

Empire, the Catholic Church became the guardian of Western knowledge. Plus, in order to calculate the correct date of Easter, the Church invested large sums of money and man-hours into studying astronomy. According to historian J.L. Heilbron, "The Roman Catholic Church gave more financial and social support to the study of astronomy for over six centuries, from the recovery of ancient learning during the late Middle Ages into the Enlightenment, than any other, and, probably, all other, institutions."[48]

The Crusades and the Inquisition

These historical events are not examples of the Church trying to forcibly convert or oppress anyone who dissented from its teachings. The Crusades were the opposite, as the Crusaders risked life and limb to rescue Christians who had been subjugated by Muslim invaders. Similarly, the inquisitions were actually more humane than secular courts of the time, and their goal was to expose individuals who threatened to undermine the general social order itself. For a thorough refutation of the myths associated with these events, see Steve Weidenkopf's book *The Glory of the Crusades* and Edward Peters's book *Inquisition*.

Complicity in the Holocaust

Some critics claim that Pope Pius XII was, at best, too timid in his denunciation of Hitler. At worst, he was involved in the systematic murder of millions of people. The truth is that Pope Pius XII acted heroically in standing up to the Nazis. Myths about his cowardice or complicity come from a piece of Soviet propaganda written in 1963 called *The Deputy*. According to Rabbi David Dalin, author of the book *The Myth of Hitler's Pope*, "Eugenio Pacelli [the future Pope Pius XII] was one of Hitler's earliest and most consistent critics and . . . as both the Vatican secretary of state and subsequently as pope, was in fact a friend of the Jewish people who was instrumental in rescuing and sheltering a great many Jews from the clutches of the Nazis."[49]

15. How can you trust the Catholic Church after its cover-up of the sex abuse scandal?

In 2002, the *Boston Globe* released an investigative series on allegations of sex abuse within the Boston archdiocese. The story led to the revelation that members of the clergy, in Boston and, as was eventually revealed, in many other dioceses, moved priests who had been accused of sexual misconduct to other parishes, which allowed priests who were guilty of abuse to continue harming minors.

This is certainly tragic, but it would be a mistake to leave the Church over this scandal, because it does not disprove the Church's divine foundation. Just as a Protestant would not abandon Jesus because of

Judas's failures, Catholics should not abandon Peter or his successors because of the failures of those they've ordained.

We must also be wary of false narratives being spread about Catholic sexual abuse that are designed to slander the Church. These narratives usually contain one of the following myths:

Myth #1: A large percentage of Catholic priests have been accused of abuse.

According to the John Jay College of Criminal Justice, about 4 percent of priests who served between 1950 and 2002 have been accused of sexual abuse.[50] This is unacceptable for any profession, but it is not unusually high among the male population. Ernie Allen, the director of the National Center for Missing and Exploited Children, said in an interview with *Newsweek* magazine, "We don't see the Catholic Church as a hotbed of this or a place that has a bigger problem than anyone else. I can tell you without hesitation that we have seen cases in many religious settings, from traveling evangelists to mainstream ministers to rabbis and others."[51]

The *Newsweek* article also reported that insurance companies that cover sexual abuse claims as part of their liability insurance do not charge higher premiums for the Catholic Church. In other words, they don't think children in Catholic churches and schools are in more danger than children who belong to other religious institutions. In fact, according to Hofstra University researcher Charol Shakeshaft, "the physical sexual abuse of students in [public] schools is likely more than 100 times the abuse by priests."[52]

Myth #2: Requiring priests to be celibate leads to child sexual abuse.

According to the textbook *Sex Crimes: Patterns and Behaviors*, "Many pedophiles of all types have adult sexual outlets. Many are married. Some have been known to marry women with children in order to have access to the children" (117). Stanford University professor of psychiatry Thomas Plante says, "Many men who don't have sex for a variety of reasons (e.g., no suitable partners, marital or relationship distress) don't turn to children for sexual gratification. They turn to other consenting adults."[53]

To put it simply: If an adult is sexually attracted to minors, he is a danger to children even if he has access to adult relationships. If he is not attracted to minors, being celibate will not cause him to develop such an attraction. The existence of abuse perpetrated by married athletic coaches, Protestant pastors, and Jewish rabbis shows that celibacy is not the reason for sex abuse cases in the Catholic Church.

Myth #3: The Catholic hierarchy was engaged in a massive conspiracy to cover up priests' abuse of children.

Most accusations of sexual abuse among priests stem from incidents that took place between 1950 and 1980. According to Monica Applewhite, who has spent over twenty years studying abuse and how to help institutions prevent it, "from the 1950s to the 1980s, these treatment-based interventions for sexual criminals [instead of incarceration] were not only enormously prevalent in the United States, but surveys of ordinary citizens showed that they were enormously popular."[54]

It was thought that the urge to commit sexual abuse could be treated with therapy, so involving law enforcement was not always necessary. Unfortunately, some Church leaders failed in their responsibility to deal with suspected priests "in house," which led to disastrous reassignment decisions that allowed those priests to abuse others. However, the Church has instituted a wide-ranging set of reforms to prevent crimes like this from happening in the future, which brings us to our last myth.

Myth #4: The Catholic Church doesn't care about protecting victims of abuse and just wants these allegations to go away.

Since 2002, the Catholic Church has taken dramatic

steps to increase transparency and accountability in the area of reporting sexual abuse. The Church has created offices of safe environment and child protection that have trained millions of adults to recognize signs of abuse. Dioceses around the world have instituted zero-tolerance policies that require immediate reporting to law enforcement of alleged abuse.

In 2015, Pope Francis created a special tribunal for disciplining bishops who had been negligent in their response to allegations of abuse.[55]

According to David Gibson, who writes for the *Religion News Service*, "The Catholic Church may be the safest place for children. Whatever its past record, the Catholic Church in the U.S. has made unparalleled strides in educating its flock about child sexual abuse and ensuring that children are safe in Catholic environments."[56]

16. Why can't married men be priests?

Clerical celibacy is not a doctrine of the Church, but a discipline that developed over time in accordance with what God has revealed in Sacred Scripture and Sacred Tradition. The Western church once ordained married men to the priesthood (and still does so today among converts from Eastern and Anglican churches). Eastern Catholic churches, such as those that celebrate Byzantine and Maronite liturgical rites, regularly ordain married men. However, their bishops must be unmarried, and an unmarried Eastern priest cannot marry after he is ordained (even if he was once a married priest whose wife later died).[57] The *Catechism* explains:

> All the ordained ministers of the Latin church, with the exception of permanent deacons, are normally chosen from among men of faith who live a celibate life and who intend to remain *celibate* "for the sake of the kingdom of heaven." . . . In the Eastern churches a different discipline has been in force for many centuries: while bishops are chosen solely from among celibates, married men can be ordained as deacons and priests. This practice has long been considered legitimate; these priests exercise a fruitful ministry within their communities (1579–1580).

Biblical examples of living a celibate life can be seen in the prophets Elijah and Jeremiah; apostles such as St. Paul; and, of course, our Lord, whose only bride is the Church. Jesus even said, "There are eunuchs [people incapable of sexual intercourse] who have made themselves eunuchs for the sake of the kingdom of heaven" (Matt. 19:12). *The Catholic Commentary on Holy Scripture* says Jesus was encouraging voluntary abstinence from sexual relations, "not by self-mutilation but by self-denial."[58] Paul affirmed the goodness of marriage, but he also wished that all could be celibate like him (1 Cor. 7:7). That's because, according to him, the unmarried are able to completely focus on pleasing the Lord without being encumbered by the responsibility of caring for a family (1 Cor. 7:32).

In the early Church, many men who were called to the priesthood were already married. Matthew 8:14 describes St. Peter as having a mother-in-law, though Peter's wife may have been deceased by that point in his life, as she is not mentioned in the New Testament.[59] However, the regional councils of Elvira and Carthage in the fourth century did mandate continence for priests, including abstaining from marital relations. Canon 33 of the Council of Elvira said, "Bishops, presbyters, deacons, and others with a position in the ministry are to abstain completely from sexual intercourse with their wives and from the procreation of children. If anyone disobeys, he shall be removed from the clerical office."

Some Protestants object to priestly celibacy and say it violates 1 Timothy 3:1, which says, "A bishop must be above reproach, the husband of one wife," and 1 Timothy 4:2-4, which says those who "who forbid marriage" teach "doctrines of demons." But the Church does not forbid marriage, because any man is free to pursue the vocation of marriage or the vocation of the priesthood. Once a man becomes a priest, however, he is expected to keep the vow of celibacy he made, just as a man who becomes a husband is expected to keep the vow of monogamy he made. Moreover, Jesus himself "forbade marriage" for anyone who had a living spouse, even if he was legally divorced (Matt 19:9). Surely, Jesus Christ did not teach demonic doctrines!

With regard to 1 Timothy 3:1, this passage does not mean that a bishop must be married; otherwise, widowed bishops would have to be removed from office. Such a requirement would preclude even Jesus, whom Scripture in one translation calls the "Shepherd and Bishop of our Souls," from the office of bishop (1 Pet. 2:25, KJV). Instead, this passage means either that a bishop cannot have *more* than one wife at a time or he must never have remarried after the death of a spouse.[60] Paul did not condemn celibacy, since, even though he affirmed a widow's freedom to remarry in general (Rom. 7:2–3), he rebuked widows who remarried in violation of "their first pledge" (1 Tim. 5:12). This condemnation must refer to some kind of voluntary vow of celibacy these women undertook after they became widows.

Far from being an arbitrary hurdle, priestly celibacy is a sign to a world obsessed with carnal pleasure that shows how God is stronger than our base desires. The celibate priest, dressed in black to signify his death to the world, is able to live a joyful life in Christ as a servant to God's people. The *Catechism* puts it well: "Called to consecrate themselves with undivided heart to the Lord and to 'the affairs of the Lord,' they give themselves entirely to God and to men. Celibacy is a sign of this new life to the service of which the Church's minister is consecrated; accepted with a joyous heart celibacy radiantly proclaims the reign of God" (1579).

17. Why can't women be priests?

Before we examine the idea of female ordination, we must remember that the priesthood is not a job the Church created. Instead, the priesthood is a gift God gave the Church so that his children would always have access to the sacraments. According to the *Catechism*:

> No one has a *right* to receive the sacrament of holy orders. Indeed no one claims this office for himself; he is called to it by God. Anyone who thinks he recognizes the signs of God's call to the ordained ministry must humbly submit his desire to the authority of the Church, who has the responsibility and right to call someone to receive orders (1578).

The Church explains the male-only priesthood not by claiming that women are inferior to men. Genesis 1:27 says, "God created man in his own image, in the image of God he created him; male and female he created them." This passage shows that it is not simply men who share in the image and likeness of God;

women share this honor. In fact, God's eternal wisdom is personified as a woman (Prov. 8), and in Galatians 3:28, Paul says that in Christ, there is no difference in value between men and women. At the end of his letter to the Romans, the apostle refers to various women who acted as co-workers with him in the field of evangelization. The Church even recognizes that the one creature who deserves to be praised more than any other is a woman—Mary, the Mother of God.

This does not contradict the Church's practice of imitating Christ, who selected only men to be apostles. Men and women are equal in dignity, but they are not identical, so it makes sense that God may call each to different vocations.

Some people say Jesus chose only men to be apostles because that was expected in the culture of his time, but Jesus routinely flouted the cultural sensitivities of his day. Moreover, outside Judea, priestesses were common in ancient mystery religions, yet St. Paul firmly taught that women could not have the same leadership positions in the Church as men (1 Cor. 11:35).

Others critics say the early Church had deaconesses, so it would not violate sacred tradition for the Church to ordain female priests. However, the Church teaches that the offices of bishop, priest, and deacon belong to the sacrament of holy orders and that only baptized men can receive these orders (CCC 1554). Deaconesses, on the other hand, were always counted among the laity and were never considered a part of the sacrament of holy orders.[61] According to the *Historical Dictionary of Catholicism*, "[Deaconesses'] ministry was chiefly to women: they cared for poor and sick women, helped in the preparation of women for baptism, and played a major role in the baptism of women (for reasons of propriety due to baptismal nudity)."[62]

Unlike the discipline of priestly celibacy, the male priesthood is a doctrine infallibly taught by the Church and so cannot be changed. This does not mean that the Church *won't* change this teaching; it means that the Church is *incapable* of changing it, since this truth follows from what is revealed in Sacred Scripture and Sacred Tradition.

In 1994, Pope John Paul II explained the issue in the apostolic letter *Ordinatio Sacerdotalis* (On Priestly Ordination), where he made this statement:

> Although the teaching that priestly ordination is to be reserved to men alone has been preserved by the constant and universal tradition of the Church and firmly taught by the Magisterium in its more recent documents, at the present time in some places it is nonetheless considered still open to debate, or the Church's judgment that women are not to be admitted to ordination is considered to have a merely disciplinary force. Wherefore, in order that all doubt may be removed regarding a matter of great importance,

> a matter which pertains to the Church's divine constitution itself, in virtue of my ministry of confirming the brethren (cf. Luke 22:32), I declare that the Church has no authority whatsoever to confer priestly ordination on women and that this judgment is to be definitively held by all the Church's faithful.

In the following year, the Congregation for the Doctrine of the Faith issued a statement that said that this teaching "requires definitive assent, since, founded on the written Word of God, and from the beginning constantly preserved and applied in the tradition of the Church, it has been set forth infallibly by the ordinary and universal Magisterium."[63]

18. What does the statement "there is no salvation outside the Church" mean?

Extra ecclesiam nulla salus is a Latin phrase that means "outside the Church there is no salvation." It first appeared in the writings of St. Cyprian of Carthage in the third century, and is often quoted in the writings of both medieval and modern popes. In 1215, the Fourth Lateran Council taught, "There is one Universal Church of the faithful, outside of which there is absolutely no salvation."[64]

Many people think this statement means that only practicing Catholics will go to heaven, but the

Church teaches that God desires the salvation of all people (1 Tim. 2:4) and so it is possible for non-Catholics to be saved. God would not close off the possibility of salvation to someone who, through no fault of his own, is not united to Christ through the Church. According to the *Catechism*, "there is no salvation outside the Church" means that "all salvation comes from Christ the Head through the Church, which is his Body" (846).

Salvation comes not from purely human religious figures such as Buddha and Muhammad, nor does it come from purely human works of charity. Jesus told us that no one can come to the Father except through him (John 14:6), and St. Peter said of Jesus, "There is salvation in no one else, for there is no other name under heaven given among men by which we must be saved" (Acts 4:12).

However, acknowledging that Christ is the only *objective* way we are saved, or that only Christ takes away the sins of the world, does not mean that a person cannot be saved if he does not know this truth about Christ. For example, one could say that antivenin is the only way to be saved from a snakebite, but a child receiving antivenin does not have to know this truth in order to be saved from the bite. Similarly, a person could seek after "the way" or "the truth" and strive to act with perfect charity without realizing he is seeking after Christ, who, unbeknownst to him, is "the way, and the truth, and the life" (John 14:6).

The Second Vatican Council considered the salvation of those who, through no fault of their own, do not have faith in Christ or are not baptized. For example, prior to the time of Columbus, Native Americans had no opportunity to believe in Christ or to be baptized.[65] Could they still be saved? Here's what the Council said:

> Those also can attain to salvation who through no fault of their own do not know the gospel of Christ or his Church, yet sincerely seek God and moved by grace strive by their deeds to do his will as it is known to them through the dictates of conscience. Nor does divine Providence deny the helps necessary for salvation to those who, without blame on their part, have not yet arrived at an explicit knowledge of God and with his grace strive to live a good life.[66]

The *Catechism* also teaches that some people who lack faith, such as atheists, may not be fully culpable for their non-belief because "believers can have more than a little to do with the rise of atheism. To the extent that they are careless about their instruction in the Faith, or present its teaching falsely, or even fail in their religious, moral, or social life, they must be said to conceal rather than to reveal the true nature of God and of religion" (2125).

Just because a person never heard of Christ does not mean God can't reveal his truth to that person.

St. Paul said that even though the Gentiles were not given the Mosaic Law, God would still judge them on the basis of another law. He says, "What the law requires is written on their hearts, while their conscience also bears witness and their conflicting thoughts accuse or perhaps excuse them on that day when, according to my gospel, God judges the secrets of men by Christ Jesus" (Rom. 2:15–16). Likewise, even if someone never heard the gospel, its moral demands can still be known in that person's heart, and God will judge how the person responded to the truth revealed in his conscience.

However, the Second Vatican Council taught that "they could not be saved who, knowing that the Catholic Church was founded as necessary by God through Christ, would refuse either to enter it or to remain in it" (CCC 846). On the day of judgment, those who are merely ignorant of the truth will receive a different judgment from those who suppressed or denied that same truth.

19. What are the Church Militant, the Church Suffering, and the Church Triumphant?

These terms refer to the three different parts of the Church that are all united in Christ's one body. The Church Militant refers to the collection of believers on earth and is what most people assume that "the Church" is. It is called *militant* not because it is at war with the world, but because it must fight the sinful desires of the flesh and the temptations of the devil. St. Paul put it this way:

> For though we live in the world we are not carrying on a worldly war, for the weapons of our warfare are not worldly but have divine power to destroy strongholds. We destroy arguments and every proud obstacle to the knowledge of God, and take every thought captive to obey Christ (2 Cor. 10:3–5).

The Church Triumphant refers to those Christians who have died in God's grace and, as such, have been freed from sin (Rom. 6:7) and now worship God unhindered in heaven. These Christians are a part of the Church since they are a part of the body of Christ. St. Paul says, "As the body is one and has many members, and all the members of the body, though many, are one body, so it is with Christ" (1 Cor. 12:12). Since Jesus holds the keys to death and the underworld (Rev. 1:18), the dead in Christ are not separated from him or from the other members of the body. Jesus himself said God "is not the God of the dead, but of the living" (Mark 12:27). The saints in heaven, by virtue of their union with Christ, are more alive now than they were on earth.

In fact, Hebrews 12:1 provides an explicit reference to the saints in heaven having knowledge of what happens on earth. Throughout chapter 11, the author praises Old Testament heroes of the Faith such as Abraham, Moses, and David. Then, in the first verse of chapter 12 (keep in mind that the original work was not separated into chapters), the author says, "Therefore, since we are surrounded by so great a cloud of witnesses, let us also lay aside every weight, and sin which clings so closely, and let us run with perseverance the race that is set before us." From the author's perspective, the heroes of the Old Testament, which the Church will always honor as saints (CCC 61), are like members of a cosmic stadium cheering us to finish the race and "keep the faith" (2 Tim. 4:7), lest we be disqualified by our sins (1 Cor. 9:27).

The Bible even teaches us that the prayers of holy people are more effective than the prayers of less holy people. For example, after Job's friends sinned, God instructed them to have Job pray for them because Job was righteous and God would hear his prayers (Job 42:8–9). James 5:16 says, "The prayer of a righteous man has great power in its effects"—and who could be more righteous than the saints in heaven, who have been cleansed of all sin? As the *Catechism* says:

> Being more closely united to Christ, those who dwell in heaven fix the whole Church more firmly in holiness. . . . They do not cease to intercede with the Father for us, as they proffer the merits which

they acquired on earth through the one mediator between God and men, Christ Jesus (956).

Finally, the Church Suffering refers to Christians who died in God's grace but were still attached to sin at the moment of death. Even though these venial sins do not completely separate us from God, Revelation 21:27 says nothing unclean will enter heaven. Therefore, these saved souls will be purged of their sins prior to spending eternity with God in heaven. According to the *Catechism*, "The Church gives the name *purgatory* to this final purification of the elect, which is entirely different from the punishment of the damned" (1031).

St. Paul says that when it comes to the members of the body of Christ, "if one member suffers, all suffer together; if one member is honored, all rejoice together" (1 Cor. 12:26). This means that the Church Militant and the Church Triumphant are united in praying for the Church Suffering. The Church even teaches that the holiness of some can be applied to the benefit of others, including those being purified from sin after death. The *Catechism*, quoting the 1899 Douay-Rheims translation of 2 Maccabees 12:46, says, "'Because it is a holy and a wholesome thought to pray for the dead that they may be loosed from their sins' it offers its suffrages for them. Our prayer for them is capable not only of helping them, but also of making their intercession for us effective" (958).

20. How can I join or help someone join the Catholic Church?

If you or someone you know is interested in becoming Catholic, you or he should seek out a nearby Catholic parish and inquire about its RCIA program. RCIA stands for the Rite of Christian Initiation for Adults and has always been present, in some form, since the beginning of the Church. Acts 8:26–40 describes how the apostle Philip taught a servant of the Ethiopian queen about Jesus before he baptized him. In the second century, St. Justin Martyr described the process of being received into the Church this way:

> As many as are persuaded and believe that what we teach and say is true, and undertake to be able to live accordingly, are instructed to pray and to entreat God with fasting, for the remission of their sins that are past, we praying and fasting with them. Then they are brought by us where there is water, and are regenerated in the same manner in which we were ourselves regenerated.[67]

In the twentieth century, the Second Vatican Council ushered in a period of renewal and standardization for the process of receiving converts into the Church. These prospective converts are called *catechumens*, which means "ones being instructed."

They receive catechesis, or the "teaching of Christian doctrine imparted, generally speaking, in an organic and systematic way, with a view to initiating the hearers into the fullness of Christian life" (CCC 5). In the Constitution on the Sacred Liturgy, the Council decreed the following:

> The catechumenate for adults, comprising several distinct steps, is to be restored and to be taken into use at the discretion of the local ordinary. By this means the time of the catechumenate, which is intended as a period of suitable instruction, may be sanctified by sacred rites to be celebrated at successive intervals of time.[68]

In 1972, the Sacred Congregation for Divine Worship fulfilled this exhortation and released a new rite for Christian initiation that is now known as RCIA. The rite is meant for adults as well as children who have attained the age of reason who seek to be full members of Christ's Church. RCIA is not mandatory; priests can determine if an alternative kind of formation would be more beneficial for a catechumen. Those who are encouraged to enter RCIA, however, will normally follow this process:

Evangelization and Pre-Catechumenate

Also known as the period of inquiry, this time allows

prospective converts to learn about the Catholic faith and hear the good news of the gospel.

The Order of Catechumens

An inquirer who wishes to become Catholic enters the order of catechumens. In order to do this, he is required to select a sponsor, who will guide him through the process of becoming Catholic and be present when he receives the sacraments of initiation. After selecting a sponsor, the catechumen is welcomed into the community at Mass through the rite of acceptance or the rite of welcoming, depending on whether he has been baptized. During this rite, the candidate stands before the assembly and states his desire both to be instructed in the Faith and to receive "a fuller sharing in the life of the Church." By formally and publicly expressing their desire to become Catholic, catechumens are joined to the body of Christ's faithful, though not in a complete way. This is evident in the fact that catechumens have a right to Christian burial even if they die before baptism (CIC 1983).

Catechesis and Purification

During this stage of the conversion process, the candidate is formally taught the doctrines of the Faith and instructed in how to live a holy, Christian life. This period culminates in the rite of election, in which the Church formally ratifies a candidate's desire to become Catholic. After this rite, the candidate engages in prayer and rites at Lenten Masses called "scrutinies" that prepare him for the reception of the sacraments.

The Sacraments of Initiation

The RCIA process reaches its climax at the Easter Vigil, during which non-Christian catechumens receive baptism, confirmation, and first Eucharist, and catechumens from other Christian denominations with valid baptisms receive confirmation and first Eucharist. It is a joyous occasion that celebrates how God has brought his children into full communion with Christ's "one, holy, catholic, and apostolic Church."[69]

About the Author

Trent Horn is an apologist and speaker for Catholic Answers. He specializes in pro-life issues as well as outreach to atheists and agnostics. He holds a master's degree in theology from Franciscan University of Steubenville.

Endnotes

1 *The Catechism of the Catholic Church*, 751.

2 *Letter to the Smyrnaeans*, 8.

3 Ibid.

4 *Letter to the Corinthians*, 44:1–3.

5 *Didache*, 14.

6 *First Apology*, 65.

7 J.N.D. Kelly, *Early Christian Doctrines* (New York: Harper Collins, 1978), 440.

8 For citations related to these issues, I recommend Jimmy Akin, *The Fathers Know Best: Your Essential Guide to the Teachings of the Early Church* (El Cajon, CA: Catholic Answers Press, 2011).

9 Patrick Madrid, "Sola Scriptura: A Blueprint for Anarchy" in *Not by Scripture Alone: A Catholic Critique of the Protestant Doctrine of Sola Scriptura*, ed. Robert Sungenis (Santa Barbara, CA: Queenship Publishing, 1997).

10 R.C. Sproul, *What Is Reformed Theology? Understanding the Basics* (Grand Rapids, MI: Baker Books, 2005), 54.

11 St. Irenaus, *Against Heresies*, 3.4.1.

12 St. Vincent of Lerins, *Commonitory*, 2.5.

13 Congregation for the Doctrine of the Faith, *Dominus Iesus*, 17.

14 John Paul II, *Ut Unum Sint*, 14.

15 *Lumen Gentium*, 8.

16 Angelo Amato, *Responses to Some Questions Regarding Certain Aspects of the Doctrine on the Church*, June 29, 2007.

17 Congregation for the Doctrine of the Faith, *Dominus Iesus*, 17.

18 Ibid.

19 St. Teresa of Avila, *The Way of Perfection*, 35:1. Cited in *Ecclesia de Eucharistia*, 34.

20 J.N.D. Kelly, *The Oxford Dictionary of the Popes* (Oxford: Oxford University Press, 1996), 1.

21 Didn't Peter refer to himself as a "fellow elder" and not as "pope" in 1 Peter 5:1? Yes, but in this passage, Peter is demonstrating humility that he is encouraging other priests to practice. He wrote, "Clothe yourselves, all of you, with humility toward one another" (5:5), so exalting his status would have contradicted his message. Besides, St. Paul often referred to himself as a mere deacon (see 1 Cor. 3:5; 2 Cor. 11:23) and even said he was "the very least of all the saints" (Eph. 3:8)—but that did not take away from his authority as an apostle. Likewise, Peter's description of himself as an elder did not take away from his authority as being "first" among the apostles (Matt 10:2).

22 *Theological Dictionary of the New Testament*, vol. 6 (Grand Rapids, MI: Wm. B. Eerdmans, 1968), 98.

23 John Calvin, *Commentary on Matthew Mark, and Luke*, vol. 2.

24 Craig Keener, *The Gospel of Matthew: A Socio Rhetorical Commentary* (Grand Rapids, MI: Wm. B. Eerdmans, 2009), 426.

25 Clement, *Letter to the Corinthians*, 59.

26 St. Ignatius, *Letter to the Romans*, 1.

27 Eusebius, *Church History*, 4:23:9.

28 *Epistle* 54:14.

29 Jaroslav Pelikan, *The Christian Tradition*, vol. II, 151.

30 John Paul II, *Professio Fidei*, May 18, 1998.

31 *Quanta Cura*, 3.

32 *Dignitatis Humanae*, 2.

33 Popes in both the early Middle Ages, such as Gregory the Great (590–604), and the High Middle Ages, such as Innocent III (1198–1216), condemned forced conversions. In his *Letter on the Jews*, Innocent III said, "We decree that no Christian shall use violence to compel the Jews to accept baptism."

34 See, for example, the CDF's treatment of the role of the theologian in *Donum Veritatis*, especially 24–31.

35 *Munificentissimus Deus*, 44.

36 *Christus Dominus, Concerning the Discipline to Be Observed with Respect to the Eucharistic Fast*, 13. This was later extended in the 1957 motu proprio *Sacram Communionem*.

37 Loraine Boettner, *Roman Catholicism* (Philadelphia: Presbyterian and Reformed Publishing, 1962), 11.

38 William Webster, *The Church of Rome at the Bar of History* (Carlisle, PA: Banner of Truth Trust, 1995), 95–96.

39 *Redemptoris Missio*, 52.

40 See, for example, http://www.ucgoc.com/bs2/32Lev19-23.htm. The unabridged quote can be found in chapter eight of Cardinal John Henry Newman's *Essay on the Development of Christian Doctrine*.

41 Philippe Ariès and Georges Duby, eds., *A History of Private Life: From Pagan Rome to Byzantium* (Cambridge, MA: Harvard University Press, 1992), 467.

42 *Redemptoris Missio*, 52.

43 Timothy Ware, *The Orthodox Church* (New York: Penguin Books, 1997), 43.

44 Ibid., 60.

45 *Orientalium Ecclesiarum*, 2–3.

46 Alister McGrath, *Reformation Thought: An Introduction*, fourth edition (West Sussex: Wiley Blackwell, 2012), 111.

47 *Solemni Hac Liturgia*, 19. Cited in CCC 827.

48 J.L. Heilbron, *The Sun in the Church: Cathedrals as Solar Observatories* (Cambridge, MA: Harvard University Press, 1999), 3.

49 Thomas E. Woods Jr., "The Myth of Hitler's Pope: An Interview with Rabbi David G. Dalin" July 29, 2005. http://catholicexchange.com/the-myth-of-hitlers-pope-an-interview-with-rabbi-david-g-dalin.

50 "The Nature and Scope of Sexual Abuse of Minors by Catholic Priests and Deacons in the United States 1950–2002," John Jay College of Criminal Justice, February 2004. http://www.usccb.org/issues-and-action/child-and-youth-protection/upload/The-Nature-and-Scope-of-Sexual-Abuse-of-Minors-by-Catholic-Priests-and-Deacons-in-the-United-States-1950-2002.pdf.

51 Pat Wingert, "Priests Commit No More Abuse Than Other Males," *Newsweek*, April 7, 2010. http://www.newsweek.com/priests-commit-no-more-abuse-other-males-70625.

52 Hillary Profita, "Has Media Ignored Sex Abuse in Schools?" August 24, 2006. http://www.cbsnews.com/news/has-media-ignored-sex-abuse-in-school/.

53 Thomas G. Plante, "Six Important Points You Don't Hear About regarding Clergy Sexual Abuse in the Catholic Church," *Psychology Today*, March 24, 2010. https://www.psychologytoday.com/blog/do-the-right-thing/201003/six-important-points-you-dont-hear-about-regarding-clergy-sexual.

54 "Address of Dr. Monica Applewhite to the Irish Bishops," March 10, 2009. http://www.themediareport.com/wp-content/

uploads/2012/11/Applewhite-Ireland-Address-Bishops-2009.pdf.

55 Elisabetta Povoledo and Laurie Goodstein, "Pope Creates Tribunal for Bishop Negligence in Child Sexual Abuse Cases," June 10, 2015. http://www.nytimes.com/2015/06/11/world/europe/pope-creates-tribunal-for-bishop-negligence-in-child-sexual-abuse-cases.html?_r=0.

56 David Gibson, "10 Years After Catholic Sex Abuse Reforms, What's Changed?" *Washington Post*, June 6, 2012. https://www.washingtonpost.com/national/on-faith/10-years-after-catholic-sex-abuse-reforms-whats-changed/2012/06/06/gJQAQMjOJV_story.html.

57 *Eastern Code of Canon Law*, 180.3.

58 A. Jones, "The Gospel of Jesus Christ according to St Matthew," in B. Orchard & E.F. Sutcliffe, eds., *A Catholic Commentary on Holy Scripture* (New York: Thomas Nelson, 1953), 885.

59 Some argue that 1 Corinthians 9:5 proves that Peter had a wife during Paul's missionary journeys. Karl Keating responds in this way: "The key Greek words in 1 Corinthians 9:5 are '*adelphaen gunaika*.' The first means 'sister,' and the second can be translated as either 'woman' or 'wife.' This means the phrase translates as 'sister woman' or 'sister wife,' with 'sister' indicating not a biological but a spiritual relationship." See Karl Keating, "Did Peter Have a Wife?" *Catholic Answers Magazine*, vol. 18, no. 5, May 2007. http://www.catholic.com/magazine/articles/did-peter-have-a-wife.

60 See George T. Montague, *First and Second Timothy, Titus* (Grand Rapids, MI: Baker Academic, 2008), 74–75.

61 In A.D. 325, the Council of Nicaea said, "We have made mention

of the deaconesses, who have been enrolled in this position, although, not having been in any way ordained, they are certainly to be numbered among the laity" (canon 19).

62 William J. Collinge, *The Historical Dictionary of Catholicism* (Lanham, MD: Scarecrow Press, 2012), 123.

63 "Concerning the Teaching Contained in 'Ordinatio Sacerdotalis,'" October 28, 1995.

64 Fourth Lateran Council, canon 1. http://sourcebooks.fordham.edu/halsall/basis/lateran4.asp.

65 This is barring some of the fanciful and incorrect historical claims of the Mormon Church. For more on that subject see my booklet *20 Answers: Mormonism*, published by Catholic Answers Press.

66 *Lumen Gentium*, 16.

67 *First Apology*, 61.

68 *Sacrosanctum Concilium*, 64.

69 These attributes are called the four marks of the Church and have been articulated since the ecumenical council of Constantinople in A.D. 381.

Become part of the team.
Help support Catholic Answers.

Catholic Answers is an apostolate dedicated to serving Christ by bringing the fullness of Catholic truth to the world. We help good Catholics become better Catholics, bring former Catholics "home," and lead non-Catholics into the fullness of the Faith.

Catholic Answers neither asks for nor receives financial support from any diocese. The majority of its annual income is in the form of donations from individual supporters like you.

To make a donation by phone using your credit card, please speak with one of our customer service representatives at 888-291-8000.

To make a donation by check, please send a check payable to "Catholic Answers" to:

Catholic Answers
2020 Gillespie Way
El Cajon, CA 92020

To make a donation online, visit **catholic.com**.

catholic.com